TIMES PAST

LONDON

JEROME MONAHAN

SOUTH BANK VIEW

London gains a new landscape. It's May 1951 and what had been a vista of bombsites is renewed in time for the Festival of Britain. Dominating the upstream portion of the site is the Dome of Discovery with the Skylon and the Royal Festival Hall. The Dome, designed by Ralph Tubbs, housed an eclectic series of exhibitions celebrating everything from the exploration of polar regions to outer space. After the Festival closed, the Dome, along with most of the other attractions, was demolished and its materials sold as scrap. The Dome's site is now the location of the Jubilee Gardens, near the London Eye.

MYRIAD
LONDON

Whitehall and the West End

London's West End grew up to the west of the old Roman and medieval heart of the city – a healthier and more fashionable environment for those wealthy enough to live there and also one close to the royal centre of power at Westminster. It has long been associated with the most sophisticated entertainment and services. It is here that many of London's theatres, cinemas, shops and restaurants are clustered. Whitehall is now dominated by government offices, but has had a rich history including being the site of King Charles I's execution in 1649.

Above: **Whitehall, 1880s.** At the time of this photograph, the Queen's Household Cavalry in Whitehall probably enjoyed a far more tranquil time – the days of mass tourism and cheap cameras are a long way off and apart from a few glances the passers-by are clearly intent on their own affairs. Then, as now, Whitehall is a hectic thoroughfare. The view is north towards Nelson's Column and Trafalgar Square.

Above: **London Fog, December 1952.** Shakespeare refers to London's "drooping fogge" – an effect of the polluting impact of soot particles in the air. In the 19th century the problem became ever greater thanks to unbridled industrial activity and domestic coal fires. In time they became known as "pea-soupers". The December 1952 fog was one of the worst and is thought to have caused some 4,000 deaths. A Clean Air Act was passed in 1956 but it was not until the 1960s that the phenomenon declined.

Below: **Admiralty Arch, 1950.** A seven-seater Armstrong-Siddeley limousine is "posed" with Admiralty Arch as a backdrop as part of the firm's promotion prior to the 1950 Earls Court Motor Show. The Arch itself was built in 1910 to a design by Sir Aston Webb as a memorial to Queen Victoria. Its central gate is only ever opened on ceremonial occasions. It has long outlasted the Armstrong-Siddeley car company in Coventry which ceased production in 1960.

Above: **Aerial View East from Westminster Cathedral.** This photograph shows the view over 70 years ago from the top of the Cathedral's 273ft campanile. Victoria Street points like an arrow toward Parliament Square, Westminster Abbey and the Palace of Westminster. The prominent domed building is the Methodist Central Hall Westminster which was opened in 1912 as part of the centenary of the death of John Wesley, who was the leader of the Methodist movement.

Right: **Downing Street, 1955.** No 10 Downing Street has been the official London residence of British prime ministers since 1732 when George II offered it as a gift to Sir Robert Walpole. On April 5th Downing Street is lined with both the press and the public awaiting the news of the imminent resignation of the 80-year-old Prime Minister Sir Winston Churchill on grounds of ill health. He was succeeded by Sir Anthony Eden.

Left: **Westminster Bridge, c1900.** This peaceful photograph of engineer Thomas Page's Westminster Bridge belies its colourful history. Thanks to pressure from the City Corporation and Thames watermen all attempts prior to 1750 to develop a fixed crossing between Lambeth and Westminster failed but, placated with £25,000 compensation, the watermen eventually withdrew their objections and a first Westminster Bridge was built. It was this earlier construction that was the inspiration for William Wordsworth's sonnet *On Westminster Bridge* written in 1802 – one of the most famous poems in the language. By 1823 its foundations were crumbling and this second seven-arch project became a necessity. It took eight years to build between 1854 and 1862.

ABOVE: **OXFORD CIRCUS, *c*1890.** The view of Oxford Circus photographed more than a century ago. Then, as now, it was among the most hectic of London's intersections. It was not until 1913 that the first of the four identical quadrant buildings that characterise the crossroads today was built – the others following on in 1923, 1925 and 1928. This is the view east up Oxford Street as it heads towards Holborn and Covent Garden.

ABOVE: **REGENT STREET, 1904.** Finally completed in 1825, Regent Street was part of the enormous scheme of works undertaken by the architect John Nash in one of the earliest examples of town planning. Despite the seeming elegance suggested by the image, in 1904 Regent Street was in a state of crisis with shopkeepers lamenting cramped premises and falling profits. The necessary reconstruction was halted by the Great War and it was not until 1927 that King George V and Queen Mary could mark its completion by driving in state along Regent Street's length.

BELOW: **THE HAYMARKET.** In the mid-17th century, the presence of a royal mews of stables encouraged a healthy trade at this spot in hay and straw. The market here expanded to include cattle and survived up until 1830. It was described then as a "spacious street of great resort, full of inns and places of entertainment". The latter element still survives and as well as being home to a number of important theatres, the Haymarket is the site of New Zealand House completed in 1961.

ABOVE: **HOLBORN**. The family hotel was a mainstay for visitors to London in the mid-19th century and one of the best known was Ridler's. In Crutchley's 1865 *Guide to London* it was classed as offering "a more moderate standard of accommodation" with rooms charged at one shilling and sixpence.

LEFT: **THE CRITERION RESTAURANT AND THEATRE, *c*1885**. The Criterion still has the reputation of being one of the finest dining rooms in the West End. Built by Thomas Verity for Spiers and Pond, the railway caterers, it was decorated in ancient Persian style with pillared arches and mosaics. The theatre, also by Verity, was built in 1874 as an add-on to the restaurant, and was constructed entirely underground. In the 20th century it was associated with successful plays by Ivor Novello and Terence Rattigan.

BELOW: **TRAFFIC IN OXFORD STREET, 1890.** Named after the Second Earl of Oxford, the transformation of Oxford Street into one of the most famous shopping streets in the world began in the mid 19th century and was more or less complete when this image was taken.

LEFT: **LYONS' CORNER HOUSE, LOWER REGENT STREET, 1930.** Lyons' Corner Houses were once the best known of London's restaurants providing cheap and cheerful fare served by waitresses known as "nippies". They offered refreshment on a giant scale and the one shown here on the corner of Lower Regent Street and Oxford Street was one of the largest. It opened in 1923. Typically, the Corner Houses devoted their ground floors to food retailing selling everything from hams to handmade chocolates. They also housed hairdressing salons, telephone booths, theatre booking agencies and a food delivery service to any address in London, twice a day.

BELOW: **VIEW FROM THE STRAND, 1934–5.** Strollers in the Strand in this period could enjoy a rare view of Trafalgar Square. The hotel that had occupied this spot had gone and building work on South Africa House was under way. Designed by Sir Herbert Baker, it is now one of the West End's most prominent buildings. It was the focus of anti-apartheid protests in the 1970s and 1980s. In 1991 Nelson Mandela – soon-to-be president of South Africa – waved to celebrating crowds from one of the balconies, acknowledging those that had campaigned for his release from prison.

ABOVE: **EUSTON ARCH** Until 1961 passengers hurrying for trains to the midlands or the north-west would have encountered a 70ft high edifice with its imposing Doric columns marking the entrance of Euston Station. Designed by Sir Philip Hardwick and built for a fabulous £35,000 in the 1830s, it was part of a collection of classically ornate waiting rooms, train sheds, and ticket halls. Despite a protest campaign the "Arch" was demolished as part of the station's redevelopment – much of the rubble being used to shore up the banks of the river Lea.

BELOW: **ST PANCRAS STATION AND THE MIDLAND GRAND HOTEL, *c*1895.** St Pancras lies on the site of one of Victorian London's most infamous slums – Agar Town. Its platforms had to be raised 20ft above the surrounding area to cross the Regent's Canal. The famous Midland Grand Hotel by Sir George Gilbert Scott was built between 1868-1872 and is considered one of the greatest examples of Victorian Gothic Revival architecture. St Pancras Station has recently benefited from the renovation that has turned it into the new Eurostar terminus.

RIGHT: **LOWER ST MARTIN'S LANE: THE COLISEUM.** Designed by Frank Matcham and opened in 1904, the Coliseum is the capital's largest theatre and one of the first to be lit by electricity. It was originally a variety hall but is now home to the English National Opera. A legal dispute with Westminster City Council forced the Coliseum to stop the globe that adorns it from rotating.

LEFT: **VICTORIA EMBANKMENT GARDENS, c1950s.** Three stretches of public garden adorn the Victoria Embankment on the north side of the Thames, laid out in the 1870s when the Thames Embankment was constructed as part of Sir Joseph Bazalgette's scheme of works for improving the capital's drainage systems. The photograph also shows Shell-Mex House – its river façade boasts the largest clocktower in London.

BELOW: **EATON SQUARE, c1960s.** Chauffeurs and immaculately polished limousines go well in Eaton Square – one of London's most exclusive addresses and home down the years to a succession of rich magnates and statesmen including W H Whitbread of brewing fame and George Peabody the American philanthropist. The square has also housed at least two prime ministers: Stanley Baldwin and Neville Chamberlain. Eaton Square was developed by Thomas Cubitt and took nearly 30 years to complete (1826-1855), which is one reason why the detailing on the buildings is not uniform.

LEFT: **ADELPHI TERRACE, 1952.** In the late 1760s Scottish labourers aided in their efforts by the sound of bagpipes raised the riverside Adelphi development to designs by the Adam brothers – James, Robert, John and William. Before the Terrace could be built, a system of arches and underground streets were created to offset the shoreline slope at this point of the Strand. With the construction of Victoria Embankment in the 1860s the Adelphi lost its riverside vantage and in 1936-8 the Royal Terrace Block was demolished. Today only a few of the houses survive.

RIGHT: **ALDWYCH, 1949.** Opened in 1905, the construction of the Aldwych destroyed the Gaiety and Opera Comique Theatres and old streets in what was known as the Clare Market area. The church of St Clement survived the Great Fire but was declared unsafe and rebuilt by Sir Christopher Wren.

Covent Garden This characterful area owes its name to having once been pastureland that once belonged to the Abbey or Convent of St Peter at Westminster. The area's current appearance still reflects the influence of the Italian architect Palladio as interpreted by Inigo Jones – the King's Surveyor of Works in 1627 at the time when the fourth Earl of Bedford decided to develop Covent Garden as a fashionable residential location. St Paul's Covent Garden (below) is known as the actors' church and contains memorials to Ellen Terry and Vivien Leigh. Within 10 years of being built, the enclosed piazza attracted a market and this grew in time to be one of London's greatest sources of flowers, fruit and vegetables – a reputation that would continue until its move south of the river to Nine Elms in 1973. There is little doubt that the flowerseller in Regent Street (left) photographed in 1905 would have received her supplies from Covent Garden. Below right is a 1912 image of the Floral Hall designed by E M Barry in 1859. It reflects the same Victorian love of glass and iron that would produce the Crystal Palace. The western end of the hall has, since 1980, been home to the Transport Museum.

LEFT: **PICCADILLY CIRCUS, 1938.** The name Piccadilly derives from *pickadil* – a kind of firm collar popular at court in the early 17th century. They were the source of tailor Robert Baker's fortune, which enabled him to invest in land and a substantial hall just to the north of today's Piccadilly Circus. The integrity of this elegant circular intersection where Regent Street meets Piccadilly has been eroded over the years first by the creation in the 1880s of Shaftesbury Avenue and then by the discovery in the early 1900s by businesses to the north-east of the loophole in their leases that made it possible for them to raise large illuminated commercial signs. Of course, the signs by 1938 were a part of the landscape and continue to make this one of the busiest and gaudiest night-time spaces in London.

BELOW: **MAYFAIR, SHEPHERD MARKET, 1951.** Architect and builder Edward Shepherd was responsible for laying out the network of narrow streets and alleys in this part of Mayfair in 1735. It was here that the sometimes riotous May fairs occurred from which the whole area derives its name. Shepherd Market has long had an association with prostitution and scandal. In the 1920s the area was an ultra fashionable address for many of London's artistic community including Michael Arlen, author of *The Green Hat*, later a Broadway hit and film.

LEFT: **MAYFAIR, JUNCTION OF CHARLES STREET AND CHESTERFIELD STREET, 1951.** A Mayfair address has long been the height of social success, and one of Mayfair's most desirable streets, still preserving its Georgian elegance, is the one named after Phillip, the 4th Earl of Chesterfield. Beau Brummel the famous Regency dandy lived at number 4 and the writer Somerset Maugham lived at number 6 from 1911-19. Mayfair itself derives its importance from being the site of the fair that was formerly held at the Haymarket. The area's development in the late 17th and 18th centuries is said to have shifted the centre of gravity of aristocratic London away from Covent Garden.

LEFT: **CARNABY STREET, 1966.** In the 1960s Carnaby Street in the West End became synonymous with swinging London – epitomised in this shot by a trendy young man posing in a cloak next to a sports car. The entrepreneur John Stephen revolutionised men's fashion and by the mid 60s the street was full of independent men's boutiques. The name Carnaby Street derives from Karnaby House, built here by bricklayer Richard Tyler in 1681. Many of its first inhabitants were Huguenots who had fled religious persecution in France.

The City

The square mile that comprises the City of London has enjoyed continuous settlement since the Roman occupation of Britain in AD43. It experienced a period of decline for nearly 200 years when they withdrew but its fortunes revived with the building in 604 of the first St Paul's by Ethelbert. The Tower of London (1078) was William the Conqueror's powerful statement that the Normans were in England to stay. The Great Fire of London (1666) destroyed the old medieval city and led to a massive programme of works under the control of Sir Christopher Wren. Bombing in the Second World War devastated the City and since 1945 there has been a steady decline in the City's traditional industries, including publishing, replaced by the rise in fortune and importance of its financial services, insurance and banking operations.

Right: **St Paul's Cathedral, 1939.** Thames-side warehouses partly obscure the view across the river of St Paul's Cathedral. This is the fourth cathedral on the site and the third of three designs proposed by Sir Christopher Wren – the one approved by Charles II in 1675 and finally completed in 1710. One of the many legends associated with the building concerns the fragment of stone handed to Wren to mark the exact centre of the proposed dome. It was a piece of tombstone and was carved with the single Latin word for "resurrection" – *resurgam*. As well as Wren, St Paul's contains memorials to John Donne and Lord Nelson. The great naval commander was buried after a four-hour funeral on January 9th 1806. Before the coffin was lowered into the crypt sailors tore strips from *Victory's* battle ensign which covered the coffin. Despite its prominence, St Paul's escaped the Blitz relatively unscathed, but largely due to the team of volunteer watchers who protected it from damage during the bombing raids.

Above: **Tower Bridge, 1934.** *The Times* of 1816 reported that the availability of steamboats had given a lift to the whole of the Thames estuary. By 1841 there were six companies vying for passengers – and here is *The Royal Eagle* passing Tower Bridge en-route for Margate. Tower Bridge – a masterpiece of Victorian engineering – opened in 1894.

Right: **View East from Monument, c1880s.** Constructed from Portland stone and erected in 1671-72, the Monument stands 202ft above the City of London. Its purpose, to commemorate the Great Fire of London in 1666, is manifest in the flaming urn of gilt bronze at its summit. The internal stairway comprises 311 steps. Originally there was only a simple safety rail at the top but the Monument became a popular suicide spot and in 1842 it was enclosed in a metal grill. The diarist James Boswell wrote that it was "horrid to be so monstrous a way up in the air", but then, as now, the visitor is afforded wonderful views, especially to the east and Tower Bridge.

BELOW: **VIEW WEST FROM MONUMENT, *c*1900.** The western view from the Monument up-river is dominated by Cannon Street Station. It was on this site that the Hanseatic merchants that dominated the North Sea and Baltic trade had a steelyard for over 500 years until 1598. The station opened in 1866 and boasted a spectacular arch over the tracks designed by John Hawkshaw. It was badly damaged during the Blitz and underwent a facelift in the 1960s, although the two riverside columns that supported the arch still remain.

ABOVE: **THE ROYAL EXCHANGE, 1906.** The original Royal Exchange was destroyed by the Great Fire of London and fire consumed its replacement in 1838. The Classical-style building was designed by Sir William Tite. It shares Threadneedle Street with Sir Herbert Baker's Bank of England built between 1925-9. The idea of a national bank equipped to lend money to the Government emerged in the late 1690s when King William III needed funds to finance his wars against France. Inset: Bank of England (1951).

ABOVE: **THE DICK WHITTINGTON PUB AND CLOTH FAIR, SMITHFIELD, c1860.** The image reveals a City of London of surviving medieval buildings and winding cobbled streets and alleys largely swept away by the Blitz and subsequent re-development. The Dick Whittington inn had a long history on this spot appropriately serving an area associated with the annual Cloth Fair that was held here from the 12th century until 1855. Whittington was a mercer who made his fortune from trading in velvet, silk and damask and was Richard II's choice for Lord Mayor in 1397 – a position he held on four occasions.

BELOW: **THE OXFORD ARMS, 1870.** This 17th century galleried inn was located in Warwick Lane near St Paul's and just adjacent to the Old Bailey. The first pub of this name was destroyed in the Great Fire of London and a new inn was built. Having survived that trauma, The Oxford Arms could not combat the advent of the railways in the 19th century. It was demolished in 1878. The last remaining 17th century galleried inn in London is The George in Southwark.

ABOVE: **ST PAULS CHURCH YARD, c1890S.** On this spot the most serious traitors and conspirators were executed, including those behind the Gunpowder plot. The area was also famous for booksellers – it was here that Shakespeare's sonnets and several of his plays were published and sold in his lifetime.

LEFT: **COMMERCIAL ROAD, ALDGATE, 1901.** Built in the 1800s by the Commercial Road Company eager to cash in on the transport of goods from the recently opened East and West India Docks, in 1870 the road was extended to reach Whitechapel High Street.

ABOVE: **THE DAILY TELEGRAPH BUILDING, FLEET STREET.** The imposing six-storey edifice of the elegant Daily Telegraph building still stands at No 135 Fleet Street – although the newspaper's headquarters has long since departed first for Canary Wharf and recently for new premises near Victoria. *The Daily Telegraph* was founded in 1855 and its sister Sunday title first appeared in 1961. *The Daily Telegraph* remains the highest-selling quality broadsheet.

ABOVE: **FLEET STREET, c1895.** Since medieval times Fleet Street has been one of London's busiest thoroughfares. Originally it enjoyed many ecclesiastical associations with leading churchmen choosing to live along its length. It was also the royal route to St Paul's. Appropriately, given its later associations with the sensational press, in the early modern period Fleet Street was known for its carnivalesque animal exhibitions and freak shows. But, it is for printing, publishing and bookselling that Fleet Street really gained its reputation. Until the 1980s the street was dominated by the offices of the UK's main daily and weekly newspapers. These are now all gone except for the headquarters of the news agencies Reuters and the Press Association.

LEFT: **THE DAILY EXPRESS BUILDING, FLEET STREET, 1939.** The black glass and chrome Daily Express building, at Nos 121-128 is arguably Fleet Street's most dramatic building and one of the most important examples of Art Deco architecture in the capital. It was designed in 1931 by Ellis and Clarke and its interior was the work of Robert Atkinson who drew inspiration from both American cinema and New York skyscraper lobbies of the period. Among the startling details are a starburst ceiling in gold and silver, travertine walls, a rosewood dado, deep black marble plinth, and bright metal fittings. By 1936 *The Daily Express* had the largest circulation (2.25m) of any newspaper in the world. In 1989 the newspaper group moved from this building to Blackfriars Road.

LEFT: **HOLBORN VIADUCT AND FARRINGDON STREET, c1880.** Holborn Viaduct, which connects Holborn with Newgate Street, was built between 1863-69. It spanned the steep slopes of Holborn and Snow Hill over the valley of the river Fleet, the banks of which were lined with wharves and warehouses. In 1702, the premises of the first daily newspaper – the *Daily Courant* – were established and later newspaper offices spread the length and breadth of Fleet Street to the west. Farringdon Street dates from 1737 when a road was constructed over the river. In 1765 a more robust underground channel was built. In 1841 work on the road began in earnest and in 1863 the Metropolitan Line – London's first underground railway – was driven alongside and beneath the new road.

LEFT: **BROAD STREET STATION, 1929.** Broad Street Station was built in 1865 in "best town hall style" according to designs by William Baker – one of the 19th century's main railway company engineers. By 1900 it was London's third busiest railway terminus.

Royal Ceremony

Perhaps the most significant measure of the importance to London of royalty is the number of associations, organisations and companies in the capital that boast the term "royal" in their names. Ever since William I made the Tower his power base in England, London has played a significant role in the history of the country's rulers.

The Palace at St James was the second major focus of power and influence after the civic authorities based in the City and was a key factor in the expansion of London westwards. London, as will be obvious from the images here, has also been the backdrop to royal ceremony down the ages commemorating both the highs and the lows in the Royal Family's fortunes.

Above: **Victoria's Funeral.** Queen Victoria died on January 21st 1901 at the age of 81. She had been the Queen of Great Britain for 63 years. Her cortege took an extended route through the capital on its way to Paddington. There the Queen's coffin was transferred to a train and transported to Windsor for a funeral service in St George's Chapel. King Edward VII made it known that the period of mourning for his mother would only last three months.

Above: **Abdication Crisis.** A demonstrator in Downing Street declares his loyalty to Edward VIII who had abdicated on December 11, 1936 because he wished to marry a divorcee, Wallis Simpson. Legally Edward was entitled to marry Simpson but the prime minister and his cabinet opposed the union and the Government would have probably resigned had he gone ahead and insisted on remaining king. His reputation was marred in the war by suggestions he was sympathetic to the Nazis.

Above: **Funeral of Edward VII, May 20 1910.** A busy schedule of royal visits abroad and a taste for indulgent living took their toll on King Edward VII and he succumbed to a series of heart attacks at the age of 68. His funeral was attended by dozens of Europe's reigning monarchs – many of whom would soon be swept away in the upheavals resulting from the First World War.

Below: **Funeral Proclamation of George V.** After a long period of sickness exacerbated by smoking, King George V died on January 20th 1936 at Sandringham. The body of the late king was brought to London to lie in state in Westminster Hall before it was taken to Windsor for the funeral in St George's Chapel. As the funeral cortege made its way through New Palace Yard on the way to Westminster Hall the Maltese Cross fell from the Imperial Crown and landed in the gutter. The new king, Edward VIII, saw the incident and wondered whether this was a bad omen for his reign.

Left: **Royal Wedding.** Princess Elizabeth marries Philip, Duke of Edinburgh, in Westminster Abbey on November 20th, 1947. This was the first time a royal wedding was filmed for television. The photograph is by Bert Hardy – one of the top photographers of his generation.

Above: **The Coronation, June 2 1953.** Crowds line Pall Mall and Trafalgar Square. It is estimated that three million people thronged the streets of London to watch the 25-year-old newly crowned Queen Elizabeth II as she toured the city following her coronation in Westminster Abbey. To these numbers must be added the many millions more who watched the events on television. The ceremony was followed by an RAF fly-past following the route of the Mall and a firework display over the Thames.

Right: **The Coronation.** Queen Elizabeth walks down the nave of Westminster Abbey following her coronation in front of more than 8,000 guests, including prime ministers and heads of state from around the Commonwealth. The ceremony required her to take the Coronation Oath which binds her to serving her people and maintaining the laws of God. After being handed the four symbols of authority – the orb, the sceptre, the rod of mercy and the royal ring of sapphire and rubies – the Archbishop of Canterbury, Dr Geoffrey Fisher, placed St Edward's Crown on her head to complete the ceremony. The hall then resounded to a shout of "God Save the Queen" while gun salutes rang out over London and its cheering crowds.

Above: **George VI Lies in State.** Guarded by Horseguards and Beefeaters, the body of King George VI lies in state prior to his funeral in Westminster Hall on Febuary 15th, 1952. It is a site long associated with ceremony being the only part of the original 11th century palace built during the reign of Edward the Confessor to survive. Originally a banqueting space, it became the centre of Government outside the City walls. It was here that Charles I was tried and condemned in 1649.

Right: **Royal Mourning.** Left to right: the future Queen Elizabeth the Queen Mother, Queen Elizabeth II and Princess Margaret Rose wearing veils during their journey between Sandringham and Windsor to attend the funeral of King George VI. His death in his sleep on February 6th followed a lung operation from which he had never truly recovered. His reign paralleled an extraordinary period of history including the Second World War. George VI endeared himself to Londoners by refusing to leave the capital during the Blitz – remaining in Buckingham Palace which suffered bomb damage on at least nine occasions. In 1940 the King instituted the George Cross and George Medal, to be awarded for acts of bravery by ordinary citizens.

London at War

"The Blitz" descended on London for the first time on September 7th 1940 – a direct reprisal ordered by Hitler for air raids on German cities. It was the start of 57 continuous nights of bombing that would kill over 15,000 people in the capital and destroy and damage over 3.5 million houses. Among the worst tragedies of the 1940-41 Blitz were the direct hits on Balham and Bank tube stations which cost the lives of hundreds sheltering below ground.

Above: **Moving Home, September 7 1940.** Members of the Home Guard help East End residents to remove furniture and other personal belongings from their bomb-damaged homes. The East End with its docks and factories was particularly badly hit.

Inset: **Royal Visit, April 23 1941.** The refusal of King George VI and Queen Elizabeth to leave London during the Blitz greatly endeared the royal family to Londoners. They made a number of well-publicised visits to the East End to meet air raid victims and inspect the damage. Despite the hardships, the bombing of London and other British cities is thought to have hardened the population's resolve.

Above: **Night Watch, November 14 1942.** This photograph by Bill Brandt shows fire guards on the roof of the Houses of Parliament. The Palace of Westminster was damaged 11 times during the Blitz – most disastrously on May 10th 1941 when high explosives rained down from some of the 500 German aircraft overhead.

Right: **Tower Bridge, September 8 1940.** Despite repeated damage in the Blitz, the Port of London continued to function. Fire-watchers worked on a rota in private and public buildings reporting fires and putting out incendiary devices they could reach in time.

Right: **Work as Usual.** It is remarkable how few firms and businesses moved their offices and factories out of London during the Blitz apart from those that were actually bombed out. The original caption to this photograph celebrated the spirit of defiance and adaptability that Londoners manifested during those dark months when Britain's fortunes really hung in the balance. It read: "Work as Usual – Mrs Marsh works amongst the broken glass of a tailor's in the East End of London."

Above: **Houses of Parliament, 1943: Downed Messerschmitt.** In many ways the most crucial stage of the Battle of Britain was already over when the Luftwaffe decided to switch its attacks away from airfields and against London on September 7th, 1940. This enabled the RAF to recover some of its strength. London was at the very limit of the German fighters' range which meant they could only offer a few minutes of support to the bombers which were then vulnerable to British fighters such as the Hurricane and the Spitfire. The latter proved superior to the key German fighters the Messerschmitt Bf 109E and Bf 110 in the many dog-fights that took place in the skies above southern England and over London.

Above: **Doomed East End, 1946.** Children play on an East End bombsite in another iconic image by Bill Brandt. It was a shot that could have been taken in any of the damaged cities and towns across Europe immediately after the War.

Left: **Farming Firemen, June 1942.** In October 1939 the Ministry of Agriculture launched one of its most famous public information campaigns. "Dig for Victory" struck a significant chord and by 1943 over a million tons of fruit and vegetables were being grown in gardens and allotments. Here *Picture Post* caught off-duty firemen at work on their allotments amidst the ruins of the City of London. St Paul's Cathedral can be seen in the background.

Sport and Leisure

London is the sporting capital of the nation. Its football clubs are among the country's most successful, its two Test cricket grounds – Lords and the Oval – rank among the best in the world and Wimbledon remains the leading event on the international tennis circuit. The capital city is the first choice for the staging of prestigious events and fixtures such as the FA Cup Final, and has been the setting for two historic Olympic Games.

Above: **Crystal Palace, April 25, 1914.** Four months before the First World War probably engulfed these young men's lives, they enjoy a carefree albeit precariously balanced afternoon's entertainment at the Burnley v Liverpool FA Cup Final held at Crystal Palace in south London. Burnley won the tie 1-0. The goal was scored by the former Everton player Bert Freeman. The game was the last ever final at Crystal Palace and was the first ever to be played in front of a reigning monarch, George V. Neither club had reached the FA Cup Final before. More than 72,000 spectators attended the match.

Above: **Oval crowds, 1905.** The Oval cricket ground in Kennington, south London, is the home of Surrey County Cricket Club and has traditionally been the venue for staging the last matches in any Test series being held in the UK. In 1905, the Australians were on a nationwide tour and took on Surrey on two separate occasions. The three-day match in May was a draw and the second in July saw the Australians win by 22 runs. The Oval was originally a market garden and as a stadium has hosted many sports including rugby and football. In the Second World War it was used as a prisoner of war camp.

Left: **Derby Day, 1900.** Derby Day in June is one of the key events in the summer sporting calendar and one that sees huge crowds of all classes and backgrounds departing for Epsom from London by train from Waterloo Station. In 1900 the Derby was won by Diamond Jubilee owned by the Prince of Wales – later Edward VII.

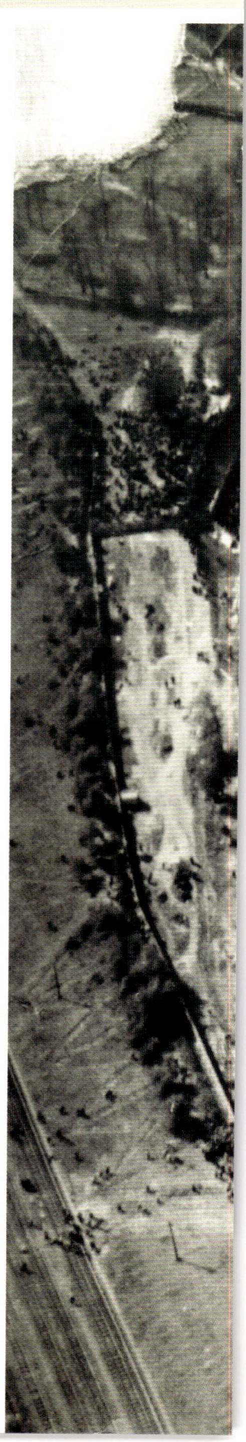

LEFT: **DENIS COMPTON, JANUARY 1 1948.** Ten years after scoring his first Test century as a precocious 19 year old against Don Bradman's touring Australians, Denis Compton runs out at Highbury for Arsenal Reserves against Fulham. The career of this brilliant all-round sportsman lit up the years before and after the Second World War. As a cricketer he remained at the top of his profession for almost three decades, playing 78 Test matches and scoring 123 centuries in first-class cricket before retiring after the 1956/7 season. Compton joined the MCC ground staff in 1934, was selected for Middlesex in 1937 and for England the following year. He made his debut for Arsenal in 1936 and was part of the side which won the League in 1948 and the FA Cup in 1950. He represented England 12 times during the war but never played for his country in a full match. Known as "the Brylcreem Boy" because of his advertising campaigns for the popular hair cream, Compton's admirers were left wondering what he could have achieved had the war years not intervened in mid-career.

RIGHT: **WEMBLEY STADIUM, 1923.** The twin towers of Wembley Stadium became a famous landmark in their own right but the recent re-development has removed them for ever. The original arena was first known as the Empire Stadium and was built by Sir Robert McAlpine to provide a venue for the British Empire Exhibition of 1924-5 at a cost of £750,000. Sir John Simpson and Maxwell Ayrton were the architects and Sir Owen Williams was the head engineer. It was built entirely from ferroconcrete.

LEFT: **WEMBLEY STADIUM.** An aerial view of the stadium during the 1923 Cup Final between Bolton Wanderers and West Ham reveals the overcrowding that occurred on that day. Bolton won 2-0. It was the first final held at Wembley and estimates suggest between 240,000-300,000 people attended.

BELOW: **THE WHITE HORSE FINAL.** Mounted police attempt to control the crowds before the start of the 1923 FA Cup Final between Bolton Wanderers and West Ham United. The game became known as the "White Horse Final" because of the presence of PC George Scorey and his mount, "Billy". It is estimated that another 60,000 were locked outside the gates. Billy became a legend and a footbridge near the new Wembley Stadium has been named the White Horse Bridge.

RIGHT: **LONDON OLYMPICS, JULY 1948.** London had been due to host the Olympics in 1944; with the outbreak of the Second World War the games were delayed until the summer of 1948 and must have been a welcome novelty in those drab and depressed years immediately following the end of hostilities. They were officially known as the Games of the XIV Olympiad, and were held in a number of locations across London with Wembley Stadium providing the backdrop to the opening and closing ceremonies and the majority of the athletics events. Germany and Japan were not invited to take part but some 59 nations did participate. Here we see the Olympic flag being carried past the extinguished flame at Wembley Stadium at the end of the Games – it then headed off to Helsinki for the 1952 Games.

INSET RIGHT: **LIGHTING THE FLAME.** British athlete John Mark lights the Olympic flame at the opening ceremony of the Games in Wembley Stadium. The ceremony completed, the competitions could begin with some 4,104 athletes pitting their strength, agility and stamina against one another in some 136 events. Among the most notable elements of the Games in 1948 were the string of four gold medals won by the Dutch Fanny Blankers-Coen, seen here being congratulated by Britain's Dorothy Manley following the 100m final on August 2.

ABOVE: **BOAT RACE, 1930.** Crowds gather to watch the Cambridge team ahead of the annual university boat race on the Thames. In 1839 the event moved to London, with the by now annual race taking place between Westminster and Putney. However, crowd congestion was such that another move was needed in 1845 – this time to the race's current stretch between Putney and Mortlake.

LEFT: **GREYHOUND GIRLS, 1938.** Smartly dressed kennelmaids who looked after the greyhounds at the White City Stadium stand alongside one of the specially adapted vans used to transport the animals. Greyhound racing was an American sport that became popular in England in the 1920s. It attracted huge crowds from all social classes, but the evening races made "going to the dogs" a particularly working man's pursuit. At the peak of its popularity, there were six greyhound stadiums in London.

RIGHT: **NO PUNCHING BENEATH THE BELT, 1938.** In a scene that would now cause scandal, a policeman instructs children in the "noble art" of boxing at Brownhill Road School, Catford.

RIGHT: **WIMBLEDON, 1911.** M Corbes (left) and J B Ward in action during a mixed doubles match at the Lawn Tennis Championships. The year was significant as this was the first time there were no Americans in the quarter-finals of the men's or women's singles at Wimbledon. The championships were first played in 1877 though the competition initially only featured men's singles. Ladies' singles were added in 1884. Wimbledon is an annual highlight in the sporting calendar and a source of some despair since no British player has won the men's singles since 1936 and Virginia Wade was the last British woman to win the women's singles title in 1977.

RIGHT: **WIMBLEDON, 1952.** Although the main courts at Wimbledon enjoy greater shade, the heat on the outer courts can be extreme. Here spectators to the 1952 matches put on paper hats to protect themselves from the sun. This was the year that the Australian, F A Sedgman, beat the Egyptian-national Jaroslav Drobny in a final that lasted 80 minutes.

BELOW: **LITTLE MO, 1954.** American Maureen Connolly carries off the 1954 women's singles title at Wimbledon. The shield is being presented by the Duchess of Kent. The immediate post-war period women's titles went exclusively to players from the USA. It was not until the Brazilian Maria Bueno won in 1959 that the pattern was disrupted. The men's titles also seemed to be reserved for American players but in the mid-1950s dominance shifted to Australians such as Lew Hoad, Neale Fraser, Rod Laver and John Newcombe.

BELOW: **WIMBLEDON WINNER, 1936.** Fred Perry's victory in the men's singles title at Wimbledon in July 1936 marks the last time an Englishman won the men's singles title. On all three occasions (1934-6) he was victorious he won in straight sets. Perry was born in Stockport, the son of a Labour Member of Parliament. He came to tennis via table tennis. Perry liked to discover his opponents' weaknesses before he played them. This paid off in the Wimbledon Men's Final of 1936 when Perry played the German aristocrat Gottfried von Cramm. Von Cramm was suffering from a groin strain and Perry was able to quickly overcome his opponent. The match lasted only 40 minutes and the German won only two games in the match.

PARK LIFE

LEFT: **KENSINGTON GARDENS, MAY 1 1912.** The photograph celebrates the first day the statue of Peter Pan went on display in Kensington Gardens. JM Barrie had been planning such a venture for six years, hoping to place it in exactly the spot where Peter Pan lands in the story right next to the Long Water which separates The Gardens from Hyde Park. The statue by Sir George Frampton was erected at night, in secret, and there was a notice announcing its appearance in *The Times* on May 1st. It proved an immediate hit with children and adults and has remained so ever since. Copies were made and there are now Peter Pan statues in Liverpool, Canada, Brussels, Australia and New Jersey.

BELOW: **CHISWICK POOL, AUGUST 1919.** There is a long tradition of open-air bathing in Britain and London had its fair share of such pools. Here we see bathers photographed just after the First World War enjoying the facilities at the open air baths in Chiswick, west London. Formerly an open air lido, Chiswick New Pool was converted into an indoor facility in 1991. The golden age of lido building in London was the 1930s when over 50 were built across the capital by the London County Council.

ABOVE & LEFT: **HYDE PARK.** At 340 acres, Hyde Park is the largest of London's Royal parks. It became a public space in the 17th century and its famous Serpentine was created after 1730 when the river Westbourne was dammed. Among its main thoroughfares is Rotten Row – photographed (above) in the 1880s. Its name derives from *route du roi* or "kingsway", and it became, thanks to the placing of oil lamps along its length in 1690, the first artificially lit highway in Britain. In the image (left) another familiar sight in Hyde Park is celebrated, namely a Norland nanny looking after her charges. Norland nannies are recognisable by the uniform which they still wear today.

Above: **Richmond Riverside, September 25, 1943.** In Russia German forces had just suffered catastrophe at the enormous tank battle of Kursk and Eisenhower had just declared, albeit prematurely, the defeat of Italy. So perhaps there was a feeling of security and lightness in the air that the people of London had not known for many years. Certainly nothing belies the carefree atmosphere suggested by this image of people enjoying a hot summer's day strolling next to the Thames in Richmond. It was published as a part of a *Picture Post* photo essay: A Quiet Sunday by the River.

Above: **Regent's Park Zoo, *c*1900.** The Zoological Society of London was founded in 1826 and the following year part of Regent's Park was chosen as the site to house its collection of animals. Visitors were not allowed to take whips with them but women were allowed to carry parasols and had repeatedly to be prevented from using them to poke the animals in their cages. It was here that the world's first reptile house opened in 1843 followed by the first aquarium a decade later.

Above: **Alexandra Palace, 1934.** A group of cyclists arrive for a rally and gymkhana at Alexandra Palace organised by the National Cyclists' Union. The event attracted over 1,000 cyclists. The Bicycle Union was established in 1878 with the express purpose of organising and regulating cycling. It became the NCU in 1883. It would remain the principal force behind British cycle racing until 1942 – the year in which Percy Stallard organised a massed-start road race from Llangollen in north Wales to Wolverhampton. Stallard was banned for life and responded by setting up the British League of Racing Cyclists.

Right: **Street Canoes, 1936.** Canoeists tend their boats before the start of what would become an annual event – the British Canoe Union's trip through London, along the river Thames between Greenwich and Putney. 1936 was the year in which the Union was formed out of a number of canoe clubs. Today it has over 30,000 individual members, 625 affiliated clubs and 145 approved centres.

The East End

The East End has long been an area where immigrants fleeing persecution or seeking work arrive and settle. Some found work in the burgeoning docks which developed along the river in the 19th century. Others, such as Huguenots and Jews, established the "rag trade" and the East End became famous as a place where clothes were made and sold. This was an area of dire poverty where many succeeded against the odds.

Above left: **Dr Thomas Barnardo, 1875.** This photograph of the great social reformer was taken in 1875 just five years after his first visit to the East End. The visit was made after an outbreak of cholera, and the sight of children sleeping rough particularly affected him. He set up a small "ragged" school and one of his pupils, Jim Jarvis, took him on a tour of the East End to see the conditions children had to endure. By 1905 there were 96 "Barnardo" homes for girls and boys.

Above: **Food Queue, 1912.** Children queue up for bread from a baker's cart. This was a period of great social upheaval in the East End, with both a dockers' strike and a garment workers' strike.

Middle left: **East End Nursery, 1936.** This beautifully equipped nursery school was one of many set up by the London County Council.

Right: **Outing to Epping Forest, 1931.** Children from Bethnal Green crowded onto a charabanc, eager for a trip to Epping Forest.

Above: **Chinese Shop, *c*1925.** Successive waves of immigration into the East End have enriched the area's history, and Limehouse has a long-standing Chinese population. In the 17th century Protestant Huguenots fleeing persecution in France arrived in their hundreds. In the 19th century following the potato famine it was the turn of the Irish, while the area became home to a large Jewish population thanks to pogroms in Russia and other parts of Eastern Europe.

Right: **Anti-German Feeling, 1915.** This desperate sign outside a shop captures the mood in June 1915 – a time when it was already clear the war was not going to be a quick or clinical affair and businesses with foreign names risked looting by enraged anti-German mobs.

ABOVE: **CABLE STREET, 1936.** The fame of Cable Street rests on a single day in 1936 when anti-fascist groups and local East Enders successfully blocked the route that Sir Oswald Mosley's Blackshirts intended to take through the area. The following week fascist sympathisers broke the windows of every Jewish shop on the Mile End Road as a reprisal for this reverse. The Cable Street battle was a major setback for Mosley and his supporters.

BELOW: **GANDHI, 1931.** An admiring East End crowd gathers to witness the arrival of Mahatma Gandhi in Canning Town. Instead of staying in smart West End accommodation, he chose to base himself at an east London community centre, Kingsley Hall.

ABOVE: **WHITECHAPEL, 1940.** By the 19th century Whitechapel was overcrowded and desperately poor. The presence of many different communities such as that created by the influx of Jewish people from Eastern Europe in the 30 years before the First World War gave the area a culture all of its own. In the 1880s Whitechapel enjoyed notoriety as a series of murders attributed to Jack the Ripper caused a sensation.

LEFT: **PETTICOAT LANE, 1938.** The Sunday market in "Petticoat Lane" near Spitalfields dates back to the 17th century, when Spanish, then Huguenot and later Jewish traders set up stalls selling bric-a-brac and second-hand clothes. Thronged with stalls, the market soon spread into the surrounding streets of Club Row and Brick Lane.

ABOVE: **THE KRAY TWINS, 1952.** East End gangsters Ronnie (left) and Reggie Kray, training at Klein's Gym. They were the dominant criminal bosses in London's East End throughout the 1960s. Their reign of terror ended with their arrest in 1968.

The Thames

"Sweet Thames", run softly, till I end my song..."
Edmund Spenser: The Prothalamion (1596)

The Thames and London's fortunes are inseparable. The river has long been a source of sustenance for millions of Londoners, providing food, water and transport as well as work in the Docks and wholesale markets that developed along its banks. But the very nature of a tidal river has brought its own challenges – avoiding flooding and building bridges across its wide expanse has been a priority for centuries.

Above: **West India Docks, 1900.** Opened in 1802, the West India Docks were the first of the enclosed docks built in the 19th century.

Below: **London Docks, c1870.** A cluster of small ships and barges is gathered at Fresh Wharf, London Docks. The first purpose-built docks in London was the Brunswick Dock built in 1789, but there had been harbours along the Thames since time immemorial. Following the development of the West India Docks, the London Dock at Wapping, the East India Dock at Blackwall and the Surrey Docks at Rotherhithe were constructed creating the largest set of wet docks in the world.

Above: **Lambeth Bridge, 1938.** Workers unloading a timber barge on the banks of the Thames with the Houses of Parliament in the background. The first mention of a river crossing at this spot occurs in 1513 with a reference to a horse ferry. This same ferry sank on a number of celebrated occasions – Oliver Cromwell's coach and horses sank in 1656. The original Lambeth Bridge went up in 1862, but was replaced by the present five-span steel arch construction in 1929-32.

Right: **London Docks, Isle of Dogs, 1889.** Writing in his diary in 1665, Samuel Pepys complained that the Isle of Dogs was a chill and uncomfortable place. It is a low-lying "U"-shaped peninsula that was deserted until a chapel was built there in the 14th century. Despite land reclamation in the 17th century, the "island" was still an exceedingly damp and miserable place in the 19th century. Its population grew insular thanks to the isolation and neglect they experienced and "off-islanders" were until recently referred to as "foreigners". In 1970 the Islanders declared "UDI" from the council.

ABOVE: **BILLINGSGATE, *c*1890S.** For centuries, Billingsgate and Queenhithe were the main wharves for the unloading of fish. Billingsgate porters famously wore leather helmets called "bobbers", said to be modelled on the headgear worn by English archers in the 100 Years War. In 1982 the fish market moved from the City to a new home in the East End.

BELOW: **WAITING FOR WORK, 1931.** There was no guarantee of work in the docks – employment was traditionally given on a first-come-first-served basis.

BOTTOM: **IN BERTH, 1955.** The Dutch ship *Lingstroom* is covered in snow at Hay's Wharf in the Pool of London during a blizzard. The Wharf was begun in 1651 by Alexander Hay and formed part of the area known as "London's larder" because of the huge amounts of foodstuffs landed here. It was particularly associated with the arrival of coffee, cocoa and tea.

Above: **London on Sea, 1939.** In 1934 George V decreed that the foreshore at Tower Bridge should be available to the children of London forever. It was such a roaring success that between 1934 and 1939 over 500,000 people visited London's "seaside".

Below: **Greenwich, 1928.** The foreshore in front of Sir Christopher Wren's Royal Naval College at Greenwich was also a popular spot for children wanting to paddle.

Above: **Under Weigh, 1930.** Two very different vessels sail together on the Thames near Tilbury. It was maritime law that all vessels of machine power give way to sailing vessels. Tilbury Docks, which opened in 1886, were a response to the steady decline in the fortunes of the West and East India Dock Company which decided to open these new docks in order to capture business from larger modern ships that could not make their way further upstream when the tides were against them. The docks at Tilbury only proved a commercial success when they were taken over by the Port of London Authority and gained a huge passenger landing stage.

Right: **The Prospect of Whitby, 1939.** London's oldest riverside pub, the original Prospect of Whitby was built in 1520. It was known then as The Devil's Tavern because of its associations with smuggling and thieving. Samuel Pepys was a regular and other famous visitors included Dickens and the painters Turner and Whistler. The pub gained its name thanks to a boat, *The Prospect of Whitby*. Moored off the tavern, it became its landmark.

ABOVE: **PUTNEY BRIDGE, *c*1860.** This early image entitled *Putney Bridge on the River Thames in Winter* was taken by Colonel H W Verschoyle and appears to show ice on the river. The Church of All Saints, Fulham, has stood on the north bank of the river for more than 900 years. The first Putney Bridge was a wooden construction built in the late 1720s. Until the opening of Westminster Bridge, it was the only river crossing west of London Bridge. The original multi-span construction was replaced by the current five-span granite bridge in 1882-6 designed by Sir Joseph Bazalgette. Since 1845 it has marked the starting point of the Oxford and Cambridge boat race.

RIGHT: **CHEYNE WALK, CHELSEA, 1951.** "River Dwellers Under Threat" – the original caption to this image reported that converted barges and houseboats moored alongside the banks of the Thames at Chelsea were under threat thanks to major embankment works. Evidently the moored homes had survived one plan to build flats on this spot. Cheyne Walk itself has had a number of famous residents including Hilaire Belloc, the painter Whistler and Isambard Kingdom Brunel.

ABOVE: **BATTERSEA POWER STATION, 1954.** This landmark building is arguably the greatest masterpiece in London of its architect, Sir Giles Gilbert Scott. The first building was opened in 1933 but the full plant did not become operational until 1953. The fumes that used to issue from the chimneys were white because efforts had been made to remove the sulphur and other impurities from the smoke – part of the attempt to reduce pollution in London. The building closed in 1983 and its future is still uncertain.

The South Bank

Southwark boasts one of the capital's oldest communities. The area was slow to develop – it was low-lying and marshy compared to the northern bank. In the 16th and 17th centuries Londoners flocked here to be entertained, visiting the brothels, bear-baiting arenas and theatres that thrived here, just beyond the reach of the City of London's increasingly puritanical authorities. It was here too that many of the more noxious industries such as brewing and tanning were allowed to establish themselves.

Above: **Shot Tower and the Lion Brewery, near Waterloo Bridge, 1945.** The Lion Brewery – sometimes called the Red Lion Brewery – was built between 1836-7. It continued to operate under this name until the 1920s when it was taken over by a Wapping-based brewing company. The building was damaged by fire in 1931 and bombed in the war, being demolished eventually to make way for the Royal Festival Hall. The only reminder of it to survive is the giant lion, made from Coade stone, an artificial stone invented by Eleanor Coade, whose present location is on the south side of Westminster Bridge. The lighthouse structure is the Shot Tower. It was one of several towers throughout the country used for the production of lead shot, used in early rifles.

Above: **The Old George Inn – Borough, *c*1890.** This is the only one of London's galleried coaching inns to have survived. It stands on the site of inns dating back to medieval times but the present structure was put up in about 1676. It lost its Central and Northern wings when the railway line leading from London Bridge station was built here in 1899. It features in Dickens' *Little Dorrit*.

Left and Above: **The Elephant and Castle.** This area, also known simply as "the Elephant", is a major road junction in inner south London and is also used as a name for the surrounding district. In 1949 *Picture Post* sent photographer Bert Hardy here to capture the life of the district – commemorating in the image of the boys (left) the kind of mixed cultural community that the area boasted then and still does. Its name is derived from the first wife of King Edward I, Eleanor of Castile. Queen Eleanor had been the Infanta of Castile. To Londoners this sounded like "Elephant and Castle". The lively street scene (above) is of trams and horse-drawn traffic at the same spot in the 1890s.

ABOVE: **BANKSIDE, 1957.** The original caption ran: "The proposal to build a New Power Station at Bankside, Southwark, which has met with considerable opposition, is to be put into effect by the Government. The Station's chimney will be 313 feet high. The main objections to the development concern its spoiling the view of and from St Paul's Cathedral." How things change – now home to the Tate Modern gallery, the power station is a familiar and much-loved part of the Thames-side scenery. Here is a view of the then current power station's chimneys and St Paul's on the north bank of the Thames beyond. Designed by Sir Giles Gilbert Scott, who was also responsible for Battersea Power Station and Waterloo Bridge, the power station was built between 1946 and 1963.

BELOW: **COUNTY HALL, 1951.** The elegant six storey County Hall, with its curved facade faced in Portland stone, was designed by British architect Ralph Knott in an Edwardian Baroque style. Begun in 1911, the building was formally opened in 1922 by King George V, but the intervention of two world wars meant that it was not completed until 1958. The building is planned around a number of internal courtyards, with the Council chamber at its heart. The long river front is decorated by a crescent of colonnades with a grand ceremonial entrance in the middle. It was originally the headquarters of the London County Council. The LCC was established in 1888 and was the first Metropolitan authority whose members were directly elected by the people of London. Its responsibilities covered drainage, building control and transport and, after 1904, the building of schools. In 1964 it became the Greater London Council, which was subsequently abolished in 1986. Now owned by a Japanese company, County Hall is today a leisure complex containing hotels, an aquarium and an exhibition devoted to Salvador Dali.

ABOVE: **BERMONDSEY, *c*1880.** The half-timbered buildings in the photograph above dated from the 16th century and housed, among others, a paper bag factory. In the 19th century the area was notorious for its tenements and slums; in *Oliver Twist* Dickens describes Jacobs Island, the corner of Bermondsey bounded by Shad Thames and St Saviours Dock, with its "crazy wooden galleries" where Bill Sykes met his end.

LEFT: **WAR DAMAGE, PARKER'S ROW, BERMONDSEY, 1956.** With Surrey Docks close by, Bermondsey was hit hard during the Second World War – more than 709 civilians were killed and thousands injured. A decade after the war ended, bombsites were still a feature of the landscape.

The Festival of Britain

Described as a "tonic for the nation", in particular for Londoners who had endured such hardship during the war, the Festival of Britain was meant to offer a bit of relief and spectacle for the population. Although the main site was on the south bank of the Thames, other exhibitions were held in the East End, South Kensington and in Glasgow. The buildings on the main site were largely built in the International Modernist syle, and the Festival was timed to coincide with the centenary of the 1851 Great Exhibition.

Above: **First Festival Lights, 1951.** The river is ablaze as the lights go on to mark the official opening of the South Bank Festival of Britain Exhibition on May 3rd. While the effort was applauded there were opponents who felt that the country could ill afford the £8m price tag.

Above: **Dome of Discovery and the Skylon, May 1951.** These magnificent structures dominated the "upstream" portion of the Festival site. The Dome was 365ft in diameter and reached 93ft at its highest point. It housed a self-contained exhibition over several floors and galleries, devoted to the theme of travel with separate areas on everything from polar exploration, including live huskies brought from the Falkland Islands to space travel. The Skylon Tower became the abiding symbol of the Festival. Made from steel, this slender cigar-shaped structure was supported on cables and lit from within at night.

Below: **Waterloo Air Station, 1953.** This was the year in which British European Airways (BEA) opened its first passenger flights between London, Rome, Athens and Cyprus. To cope with the new demand, BEA closed their Kensington Air Station, opening up their Waterloo Air Terminal immediately afterwards.

Right: **The Lion and Unicorn Pavilion and the Royal Festival Hall, May 1951.** This shamelessly nationalistic element of the Festival of Britain attempted, in combination with the nearby People of Britain Pavilion, to arrive at a definition of British identity by celebrating its "realism and strength... independence and imagination". It was adorned with murals by Edward Bawden. The Royal Festival Hall was built on the site of the former Lion Brewery. In 1964, foyers and terraces were added to the front of the building facing the river and many of the building's more grand Modernist features were removed.

First published in 2008 by Myriad Books Limited
35 Bishopsthorpe Road, London SE26 4PA

ISBN 1 84746 130 1

EAN 978 1 84746 130 8

Designed by Jerry Goldie Graphic Design

Printed in China

www.myriadbooks.com